'Ugh! That looks more like the extension to the National Gallery than a carbuncle.'

'PROBABLY JUST A VIRUS'

Dickinson

back at the doctor's

Foreword by RICHARD GORDON

COLUMBUS BOOKS
LONDON

First published in Great Britain in 1986 by
Columbus Books
19-23 Ludgate Hill, London EC4M 7PD

Printed and bound by Clark Constable
Edinburgh, London

ISBN 0 86287 228 6

Foreword

I am delighted to pen a foreword to this delightful and deliriously funny book of cartoons by my distinguished professional colleague, Dr Geoffrey Dickinson, FRCP, FRCOG, BMA, etc.

Dr Dickinson's is a medical household name. Apart from being one of our leading specialists in iatrogenesis (please look up), he is deeply loved by all his patients, so much by some of the female ones that he has continual trouble with the General Medical Council.

Dr Dickinson's comedy, originality and warmth were matched only in the sixteenth century by Dr Rabelais, renowned for a Rabelaisian sense of humour, and in this by Dr A.J. Cronin, creator of *Dr Finlay's Cashbook*, and Dr Crippen, who appreciated the value of a good cellar.

Dr Dickinson has a brilliantly penetrating eye for our profession. His drawings of doctors are as amazingly accurate as they are strikingly funny. He cheerfully exposes to the public our toils, torments, foibles, failings, dodges and disasters, because only he – as a doctor – can appreciate how we *really* feel in the (extremely) close encounters that add up to medical practice.

Hang on.

Hold hard.

I have just discovered that the beastly Dickinson is *unqualified*!

How the blighter can draw all these wonderful doctor jokes when he is *not a doctor himself* is more than an outrage. It is one of medicine's great mysteries.

I shall refuse to consult him about the bilateral laparoherniation he has been causing me for years (please also look up).

Richard Gordon

3

Flying Doctor

'*Typical – no examination, just sprays the place with disinfectant.*'

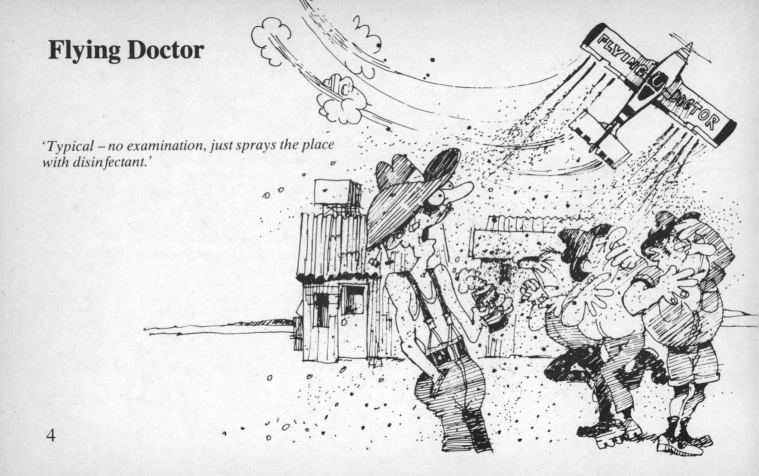

'He won't be long now – that's his receptionist
dropping old magazines to read.'

5

'Breathe in. . .
breathe out. . .'

6

'I'm just going to give
you a little injection,
Bruce.'

'Well, he would insist
on a second opinion.'

8

'Strewth, Clive –
it's the Family Planning Patrol.'

9

'Now I can't even see the plane,
never mind the letters.'

Alternative medicine

'I was right – your diet is exactly the same as George Bernard Shaw's.'

'... and you should get a nice crop of pears next spring.'

'How much elderberry wine are you getting through?'

'Nothing serious – you're jammed solid with bran and lentils.'

'Looks like an acupuncture overdose to me.'

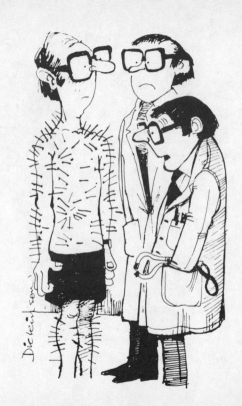

14

'Spare us a fiver for a bottle of
rose-hip syrup, doc.'

'I'd cut down on the number of protest badges
you wear – now.'

15

'Well, faith-healing hasn't done your
rheumatism much good –
can I interest you in double-glazing?'

16

'I have an alternative psychiatrist – he slaps you around
and tells you to pull yourself together.'

Doctors' D-I-Y

'Ah, to hell with it! Give it a couple of aspirins and I'll look at it again tomorrow.'

'At least the cock-ups aren't under the stitches.'

'Ring up George Fotheringay – he does by-pass operations.'

20

'It seems to be some sort of prostate problem.'

'I envy you lot – anything goes wrong
and you just blame it on a virus.'

'*The makers say we should give it more dietary fibre.*'

23

'Much better, Mr Johnson – you'll soon be able to tackle the out-patients' waiting-room.'

24

In the kitchen

'My bleeper – either I'm needed in casualty or my cake's done.'

25

‘ "Marry me," you said, " you don't want to be
a theatre sister all your life. . ." '

'That's the third lot of kidneys
I've ruined this week!'

'I ran out of sausage skins.'

*'It's a by-product of his micro-surgery –
each shrimp is filleted and then individually flambéed.'*

Conference doctors

'You'd think they'd have a by-pass.'

'Probably the Gillick family come to lobby us.'

'I'll meet you after dark in the car park
for a quick smoke and a drink.'

'Personally, I'd have made a deeper primary
incision slightly higher on the thorax.'

'*Fruity bouquet – and the good deep colour of a rhesus positive.*'

32

'*Those in favour, 40. Those in favour but would like a second opinion, 800. Those who would like to see the motion again in a week, 260. Those who do not give free consultations. . .*'

Kids' clinic

'You told me to bring him back
when he'd got all his teeth.'

34

'Ah, single-parent family –
are you the father or the mother?'

'I can't get him out
of the basket.'

'I sometimes wish I'd never persuaded my husband
to resign from the Militant Tendency.'

'That's the best I can do. If you'd like to see
another child psychologist. . .'

'Well, we'll stop the natural childbirth
exercises for a start.'

What's up, Doc?

'You'll be lucky – I'm his wife and
it's taken me a week to get an appointment.'

38

*'. . . and don't let him tell you it's just a rash –
I know smallpox when I see it.'*

'His night answering service too?'

'You mean private patients' files are mixed with those of NHS people?'

40

'Of course I could be wrong – I'm only the cleaner. The rest are all away on courses.'

'I suppose it's too late to ask for a third, fourth and fifth opinion?'

43

'First I'm going to surgically remove your jeans.'

'I once made a New Year's resolution to read the literature on what you've got – but you know what resolutions are...'

'Well, I didn't have high blood pressure before you lot got a blasted increase.'

'Nothing serious.
I'll give you
something
cheap for it.'

46

'How do you want to pay,
direct debit
or hire purchase?'

'I keep thinking I'm the Prime Minister!'

'That's funny – I keep thinking I'm a psychiatrist.'

Holiday diseases

'I got mixed up in crowd violence watching the clock golf at Eastbourne.'

'You haven't been staying in a very cheap Algerian hotel
or a National Health hospital,
have you?'

'It all started when the restaurant refused
to accept sterling travellers' cheques.'

49

'That's a nasty case of sunburn, Bishop.'

'I was in a bar outside Marseilles
and a Legionnaire trod on my foot.'

'Every time there's a drought it's the same –
people full of neat scotch diving
into empty swimming-pools.'

Peak condition

'Here's a turn-up for the books – a doctor who makes house calls.'

'I thought meths was for hardening your feet.'

53

'You do realize I've been waiting here for four hours, doctor?'

'I'd like a second opinion.'

Doctor Frankenstein

'*Dead loss as a human being –
but what a great prop-forward!*'

'It should be sent to an English boarding school where it wouldn't be so conspicuous.'

'Of course you're not illegitimate! It's just that I never got round to finishing your mother.'

'Didn't take the Japanese long to flood the market.'

58

*'Run for your lives –
Dr Frankenstein's
receptionist has
got loose now.'*

59

'Oh my God – now it's turned into a football hooligan.'

60

'Ah well – some you win, some you lose.'

Dr Jekyll and Mr Hyde

'I'm sorry, Mr Hyde, but Dr Jekyll has been struck off.'

'Oh God – it's his locum again.'

'You're lucky – Mr Burke and Mr Hare
will let you go first.'

64

'Second opinion? Come back about midnight.'

'Old Jekyll just says there's
a lot of it about.'

Doctor Crippen

'In the cirumstances, I wonder if you'd mind if I saw him first?'

'I just asked him to give me
something for the wife's
headache.'

'Nothing personal, Dr Crippen, but I thought
I'd try it on the cat first.'

*'No, no, I'm Crippen –
he's Ethel le Neve.'*

69

'As long as you're here, Dr Crippen, I wonder if you'd have a quick look at this knee of mine?'

'*To save time, Dr Crippen, you might as well sign the death certificate.*'

Nurse Nightingale

*'Get on with it – in a hundred years' time
dirty, cockroach-infested hospital kitchens
will be a thing of the past.'*

'*Damned women nurses! In the old days we'd have eaten a wounded regimental mascot.*'

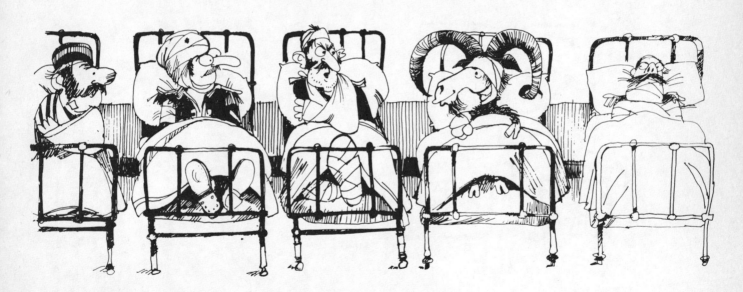

'Poor devil – Miss Nightingale dropped her lamp on him.'

'I'm afraid the officers want their table-leg back for the victory dinner in the mess.'

'You're in luck, Colonel Bogey –
guess what Miss Nightingale
found in a big high tree a mile away?'

Doctor Livingstone, I presume

'I'm sorry, Mr Stanley – Dr Livingstone's up the Zambesi doing hernias.'

'Dr Livingstone's surgery is another ten miles –
and this is the end of the queue.'

'Livingstone's bleep.'

'Well, at least we've found
his anaesthetist.'

'... but the good news is that you'll never be able to smoke, drink or drive a car again.'

Acknowledgements

Punch Digest for Doctors
Primary Health Care
Financial Times